Additiona
An Inner Light Th

"As a GP with an interest in literature, I appreciate these poems by Liz Everett and the spectrum of life that they cover: from the joy of nature, to love, faith and painful feelings of loss. I am sure that they will bring insight and inspiration to others who have the pleasure of reading them."

Tony Avery
GP and Professor of Primary Care
University of Nottingham

"When I read Liz's poems they help me to understand certain situations that have happened in my life. Giving me hope and inspiration for the future."

Lindsey Hopkins
Reiki Master Practitioner
& Anusha Master Teacher

"This is a book that can show you how to embrace your inner-self and alter your perception in a wonderful healing way. A beautiful, life-transforming book to enjoy."

Cecelia Anne Sadek
Marlow Poetry Society

"Liz shines her light with radiant simplicity, expressing both her sorrow and joy in a way that touched my heart. I felt moved, uplifted and inspired as her experiences resonated with my own, nudging me further forwards on my inner journey."

Patsi Hayes
Healer and Spiritual Mentor

"Liz has written a marvellous collection of writing and poems. Her style passes a message to the reader in a special way which touches one's emotional heart strings. Sit back and read them slowly and you will be amazed at where your dreams take you."

Reiki Student

"Liz's, passionate writing is compulsively readable. She is a master of exploring the human 'heart'. We can identify ourselves with our own complexities involving longings, hopes, search for the meaning, empathy and compassion. Her writing is brilliantly intuitive enabling the reader to read between the lines and hence sending on the profound journey of self-discovery."

Dr. Eva Carlton
Ph.D. BSC (Hons) Psychology

An Inner Light
That Shines So Bright

A Heart Warming Collection of Inspirational Writings

By Liz Everett

To Ann.

With love
& Best Wishes!.

Liz Everett.

X.

lıp

First published in 2009 by:

Live It Publishing
27 Old Gloucester Road
London, United Kingdom.
WC1N 3AX
www.liveitpublishing.com

All enquiries should be addressed to Live It Publishing.
ISBN 978-1-906954-05-5 (pbk)

Dedication

For Marian Ayling...

A wonderful woman, who gave me tremendous strength. Her positive outlook was a shining example of splendour.

Marian, sadly, is no longer physically with us, though spiritually her energy surrounds me.

Contents

Introduction

As a child, I grew up in a large, happy and loving family. When I left the family home I experienced many significant events, not knowing that this move would change my life forever.

I was diagnosed with, and treated for, cancer and suffered the effects of long-term depression.

My journey to recovery began ten years ago when I enrolled on a Diploma course to study Person-Centred Counselling, and since then I have never looked back.

During this period I trained in alternative therapies, becoming a Reiki Master Teacher, studying a new healing energy called Anusha and then later gaining a Diploma in Indian Head Massage. Alongside the healing, I worked in the Youth Service, counselling and supporting teenagers.

All these therapies opened an avenue that inspired me hugely and triggered many emotions, resulting in a need to express myself, which subsequently poured out in my writings. These emotions found expression in a poetic and reflective style. In a short time I had written over 200 pieces of writing, most of which are in this book.

I began to realise the impact that these powerful words were having upon me, my family and friends. I noticed that they contained strong and meaningful messages that had the ability to heal. I felt an overwhelming need to reach out, to help others, and this was the motivation and intention for publishing this book.

I believe this collection of inspirational writings, covering themes such as Nature, Angels, Faith and Empowerment, are both inspiring and uplifting in a variety of ways. As I was writing I found an inner peace and felt connected with the Universe and the natural world.

I feel so blessed that I have created the opportunity to write this book - I wrote from my heart and I hope that these words will touch your heart in some way. Each word, thought and feeling has been an experience of mine, and has enabled me to find my way home, finding my way back to my inner self.

I am now happily settled, living back in my home town with my partner and two children.

Finally, I've found the inner light that shines so brightly within me!

Liz Everett
Buckinghamshire, England
September 2009

Acknowledgements

My heartfelt thanks to:

My wonderful partner, Giles, without your love, support and patience this book would not have been possible. Thank you for giving me the freedom to find myself. I love you endlessly.

My beautiful children, Melissa and James, for being so loving and caring, always giving me unconditional love. You are both my shining light.

My amazing and extraordinary Mum and Dad for your love, generosity, support and understanding. For always believing in me.

My family, brothers and sisters, for the magnificent love you've shown me. You have all been an inspiration to me.

My very special friend, Helen, who is always by my side, encouraging and supporting me in all my ventures and adventures! Thank you, you will always be my friend.

My dear friend Tanya, you have the kindest heart and always show that to me, forever my friend.

My marvellous teacher and mentor, Patsi. You have inspired and encouraged me, and given me no end of amazing support. You are a remarkable person and I thank you from the bottom of my heart.

Kate, for always welcoming me into your home, for being a strong support and encouraging me right from the beginning of my journey.

All my special friends, thank you for your kind support and encouragement, for allowing me to be myself.

All the healers and counsellors that I have been lucky enough to meet and work with. It's an absolute pleasure to have you in my life!

And, of course, to my wonderful Publisher who believed in me from the very beginning, for giving me boundless encouragement and guidance. Thank you for your generosity and for making my dreams come true.

And special thanks to all those people who I've crossed paths with during my life... you have all touched my heart.

A Masterpiece

A masterpiece that you shall keep;
it's a rare and special thing.
You are unique.

Healing

When you feel stuck at a certain point in your life, and can't see a way out of it, you can feel debilitated, fatigued and lack motivation.

Sometimes a change is just around the corner, so close – yet you feel it's so far away. Often it isn't at all.

I have chosen the following poems to illustrate that you can move forward. Hopefully, they will give you faith and courage to begin making changes in your life.

How rewarding and tremendous that can be!

An Inner Light
That Shines So Bright

I connected within to hear the tune of my own music, I listened to myself and found what I needed.

To nurture, to love, to feel peace from above; most importantly to connect from within.

My energy grew, like the plants in Spring, I blossom each day to find the confidence that I'd lost along the way.

I have faith and believe in myself
to make the shift, and turnabout.

To climb out of the darkness I've felt for so long, to the lightness that was there all along.

Preserve My Energy

I build my energy bit by bit, to store my reserve, so as to preserve.

I treasure myself, so I feed myself well, I nurture and bathe and wrap myself up, just like when I was a babe.

I keep myself well, my intuition serves me well.

Summer Breeze

Summer breeze gets you through, to ease the pain
that you once knew.

As the sun shines down and penetrates through, your
body takes the healing too.

The Sea & Infinity

Life is a reflection of the sun and the sea... and I can find the beauty in me.

Golden light that shines on me to bring me love and life, so free.

Where the sea stretches out for miles and miles like life and its infinity.

As the sea laps against the shore, it's showing that I'm here once more, to gain the truth enriched with bliss.

The waves wash over and rescue me. For the tides of time are what I see, that stretch out in front of me.

A true reflection – simply me.

Time Moved On

The fears I cried were something more and, actually, I found deep from the war.

A time when I was lost and scared, I felt rejected, not accepted.

So, as time passed I muddled through and what I found was something new.

Beauty around me I relished with joy, the landscapes – my security I started to employ.

Peace stood still as time moved on and the echo of bombs had long since gone.

Luckily, so I lived on!

The Elements

If I can give something from me, it would be to love life, and treat it as treasure.

For life travels fast, and it's all in the past when the pain and the hurt was in me.

It takes time to heal, and life has a wonderful way of giving me pleasure.

Some elements of life, being water and air, give out properties that cleanse and free my soul.

Releasing all my pain and allowing me to start over again, to regain my energy; allowing my emotions to settle once more.

Shining Light

The waves were fierce and strong in the storm, like barriers to break through.

Emotional blocks, how can I break through?

Drop the fears one by one – like chipping away at the old exterior to uncover the truth.

No anger, no guilt, no shame that built.

What's left is the pureness surrounded by light, an innocence that shines through.

So bright, like a child with their spirit set free!

A Thousand Thoughts

A thousand thoughts, a thousand miles away,

not relevant to what's happening today.

Be still, at peace and in the moment.

Don't waver and let other influences knock you down.

Don't be swayed by the daily stresses all around.

Don't rush with the others.

Stay back, hold tight, keep with nature.

Don't fight life with its twists and turns,

a journey of adventure.

Believe it's good – then it turns out good.

Stay Strong

When the world is harsh stay strong and calm, stay focused and know that your reason for living is to give love, understanding and compassion to others.

Spread this everywhere, know you have faith that all will work out in the end.

Time will heal, love conquers all. Strive to reveal the truth, to act in a way to save the day.

I found comfort in my joy and peace, in my home once and for all.

Sunsets

Sunsets – a picture to hold in my memory even through the toughest times when pains endured.

The beauty resonates close to my heart, as another new day unfolds.

A sadness creeps in from time to time, but hope fills me still, for I trust in all I see and hold that dear to me.

So, I feel blessed once more to travel the fields of gold.

Peacefulness, I Cry

Sand dunes piled up high, a sense of calm,
of peace, I try.

The water sizzling fills the air.

The shores are crisp so – strong, so fair.

Another world where the North wind blows, in peace,
and makes the waters swirl.

I rest my head to breathe it in. I calm my mind...
my thoughts unwind.

I make the room to join the dunes – I sink into a
meditative state; to bring my dreams into my head.

See pictures, colours of peacefulness.
I sit and silently cry.

Mending My Broken Heart

The tears spilled from my eyes, tears of the pain I had tried to hold back, when in my sadness, there was despair.

Then hope accompanied me from the comfort of kind words of others. Others who cared and shared their experiences from their past.

I waded through and found that I too believed, that we could cure the upset, and turn around to change its course.

The choice was there for me to take and make it – or break it.

I made it, carefully putting back the broken pieces of my heart, to restore the love we all once knew.

A rainbow of light shining down on me.

Music Soothes the Mind

I sat feeling gloomy.
I couldn't describe the feelings that were stirring and starting to rise.

I wanted to grasp onto something like hope.
My mind and my body just wanted to choke, and stay with what life had brought with a jolt.

So, I gave into sadness and sacrificed hope.
I stayed with the emotions that were painful to me, but could not compare with the suffering she had to endure for a time, you see.

For now I needed something to fill this time, so I put on some music that soothed my body and mind.

The music brought meaning and peace of a kind.
The tender sweet words were powerful for me, and just for that time I drifted inside.

Love Boundless

Golden light, a delight, the sun's rays to
re-energize, makes me feel more alive.

Love boundless like reaching the stars, no limits.

Soaring through like the birds when they take flight.

Gliding gracefully, dipping, swerving, weaving in and
out.

Sky-diving with a freedom that taps into my solar
plexus.

To release my power and freedom of joy and love.

Laughter

To laugh felt so good... I'd forgotten I should. Responsibilities weighed me down with the seriousness at hand.

To laugh and have a blast just once in a while, was the best tonic I could order.

So each and every day I make it my way, to find something funny to say.

The more I laughed, the more I felt joy, and infectious to others as the house filled with joy.

My message today: 'Bring a smile to yourself & others'.

Love is...

Life took a turn that was kind of unexpected when the love of my life appeared before me.

Love has no rules. I can be whoever I want to be.

Love is kindness with no limits.

Love is blind – beauty in your eyes.

Love is safe. I never need to worry or feel insecure.

Love is when the sun shines on me and on you.

Love Shows the Way

I was patient and kind and knew that you would get through somehow. I believed this was a matter of course for you, and that you would see the light once more.

I didn't know what to make of it, and couldn't make sense of the very reason behind it all.

So, I loved you through and through,
as love conquers all.

Love Within

When I feel the darkness creeping in, I embrace myself
and speak within – kind words of comfort like I knew,
when someone else was comforting too.

My heart warms up when I think of love, and share my
thoughts with those I love.

It's All Inside

I feel an urge – a growing need, to ease the pain of those in need.

To fight the fears life has to rear, when unexpected I feel rejected.

As we move to know, and we once knew, that life is more ethereal then mere material.

Get back to bliss; don't fight with this, look deep inside and you will find your inner voice, your inner mind.

And peace and quiet of a different kind to what you see in front of you.

Colours beautiful, deep dark blue is one of those that's running through – like the rivers flowing and the waters swirling.

Rolling hills of evergreen, with peace running through like you've never seen!

Forgiveness

Forgiveness releases all hold on me and bitterness has no place in me.

My anger has no time to reside, as I let it go ever so quickly.

I feel accomplished because of this – tremendous, in fact, and very intact.

When I look at all the parts of me, I'm happy with everything that I see.

No such thing as perfect, so I don't try – I'm just so glad that this is how I want to be.

I blend in with the world I see, and have found my place in the world to be me.

Emergence

I handed back the guilt that had trapped me like a prisoner who couldn't escape.

I broke out and freed myself from the ills that had kept me in such a state.

So what emerged was a beautiful bird with their wings displaying refined intricate details. Amazing unique, shining!

Never bleak, with a personality brand new.

Cinderella

I contemplated what life should be and realised that it was dismal to me.

My ideal world had fallen apart – it wasn't the start I'd wished it to be.

Like Cinderella when she met her Prince.

Pain and sadness and suffering too were all the things I had to do. In order to make my life somehow.

To blossom and bring some peace for now.

A Sense of Peace

I've finally found a sense of peace

I can tune into it day and night

I can take this feeling anywhere I go

I can use it to my advantage whenever it's needed

I can visualise anything – the sunset, the sea, as far as
the eye can see

I've created my surroundings, inside and out

I have lost that terrible feeling I suffered long ago

I've replaced it with a warm wonderful feeling

It comes from Reiki, Anusha, the power of healing

It's because of the people I surround myself with,

that has finally helped me to come to this

I can spread this around wherever I go, now I finally
know how it feels

This sense, this feeling of wonderful peace.

Acceptance

I showed my true strength, my spine divine like the tallest trees and the birch green leaves.

With a stem so strong to hold me up, and to touch my emotional dreams.

To unravel the past, to change my path, a choice to make or stay where I was.

To expend all my energy wading through on this treacherous journey, or start anew?

To gain inner wisdom flowing through, to gracefully accept myself, and all that's new.

Nature

I found great comfort when writing about nature. I took more notice and heard the birds singing and admired what was around me more than ever before.

Walking in nature is very relaxing and beautiful at any time of the year, and brings me a sense of peace and calm that takes me away from the sometimes stressful times. This was when I could take in the beauty of my surroundings and write at my best.

The following selection has been carefully chosen to bring you peace and tranquillity.

Seasons Changing

I wondered if life is planned, or is it fate the way it turns out?

It's so amazing and special to be here, to live this life and not know how it's going to be.

To enjoy the sunsets, the seasons so changing. To watch the way the autumn leaves are ranging. Reds and golds and shades of brown, all falling gently to the ground.

To watch the snow falling... see footprints on the ground, the warm glow of lights in the windows of houses.

When spring comes the flowers are dawning, the fresh smell in the air - the birds soaring.

Spring turns into summer and rolls into one – don't know how long it will last, so I savour each day till it's past.

Round and round as time goes by... so treasure our lives as best as we can, or, before you know it, it's the end of life's span.

Close to My Heart

My energy soared out from my heart, an array of colours to display my love – prisms of colour that attracted the good.

The meaning of life had been lost to me for a while, hidden under a cloud, like a thick fog on a winter's night.

The cloud lifted and disappeared – a new way was shown to me.

Colours so strong! All shades so green of every range of beauty within, of every spectrum for my eyes to see the beauty's within me.

So within, so without – I don't have to shout as I'm heard without a doubt.

My personality shone through – and so can you when you find your way.

It's right on your doorstep, close to your heart – you'll find it when you're ready to start.

No need to fear – it's all so near.

At One with Nature

Silence filled the air, and peace stilled the air,
my emotions were intact.

The dust had settled, the sorrow had past, though the
memories were still somewhere in my mind.

I comforted myself by the smallest things.

When the leaves are swishing in the wind, whispering
in time to the rhythm in my mind.

They're calling out to welcome me,
they need attention too.

Welcome Rain

The rain poured and I saw that it was refreshing and cleansing.

The plants welcomed the rain and everything grew with pleasure.

I might not sit in the rain, but what harm would it do for me to walk through the rain?

I appreciate the ever-changing weather, when the sun shines its golden treasure, when the wind blows it catches my breath, clearing the cobwebs from my head.

And when it's cold, my body may shiver so I wrap myself up, so I don't quiver.

Whatever the day, I'm happy to say that I'm grateful for it, and adapt to it with huge pleasure.

When Winter Comes

Another exciting day approaches.

Soon the leaves will be changing, showing beauty in the trees.

The grass has stopped growing, no longer needs a crop.

The flowers resume into an emptiness, a time where they no longer bloom.

To go to sleep for winter, keep snug and warm; get ready in case of the winter storm.

Sleep quietly until its time to wake, not sorry till the dawn doth wake.

And when the winter nights have gone, the spring begins again, once more.

When all the flowers come to wake, they all look forward to the sun, to break.

We gather together the plants and me, and feel the good energy, from them to me.

I Am Thankful For Each Day

My sweet cottage high up in the hills, buried safely and secure amongst the wildlife dashing here and there.

The squirrels build their home amongst the trees, so rare.

The views are a sight to see, colours so variant and beautiful to me, and when the suns high in the sky and the birds fly playfully...

I smile and sigh as I've come this far for this sight to see.

When the moon glows and the wind blows I know and feel alive, my body responds entirely to these ever – changing sights I see.

And when I lay to rest my sleepy head, I pray for another day ahead.

The Thunderstorm

The thunder banged loudly and echoed through the
air. The pressure built and repressed the air.

The thunder clapped and the lightning flashed.
A bolt of light shot through the dark grey sky.

Then all was calm... no sound, no sound to alarm
except the raindrops beating like a drum, washing and
cleansing everything.

The plants, the trees, the flowers to ease,
the drought that had caused the storm.

The Jasmine Plant

The Jasmine plant reflected in the glass top table, and showed an image of wonder and glory.

The garden emanated a peacefulness that seeped through me. Bringing me into a new world that had always been waiting.

I had been blinded and hadn't seen before what this meant to me. Now, now, it meant even more.

And the beauty in me, brought out the beauty in you, to share amongst them all.

Replenish

The birds play a symphony that echoes through the trees – high notes, low notes that bounce back through the breeze.

I raise my eyes up, to gaze at the trees – high up in the hills that lift my spirit with ease.

My emotions were high; this sight calmed me still – brought a peace that took away the chill.

To keep control my emotions intact, I stroll to the river and then wander back.

Replenished and healthy, a vitality new – a chance to unwind and now start anew.

The Singing Birds

The birds brought me comfort. It seemed that they knew that I was sad and feeling lonely.

So they sang a tune to cheer me up, that tweeted and chirped and perked me up.

Nature to Share

The clouds merged together to show me that we too were united and strong.

The sun peeped from the clouds and brought comfort, warmth and peace.

I let my thoughts drift from my mind and disappear away, until unknown.

Reality felt far away as I reminisced... memories of happiness, and joy when I was a child.

Taken care of, no responsibilities – sheltered, fed and warm.

The sun fed my energy as I bathed and breathed in the fresh air and sweet smell of flowers.

Freshly cut grass, a reminder of special moments in the summer.

The birds joining in to bring me company when I was alone.

Nature always there for me, to enjoy and share.

My Outlook

The evergreen mountains so high,
bring tears to my eyes.

Tears of elation and happiness!
To be in this life in the glory of all that you see.

All the beauty that surrounds me.

Gold tipped mountains that my eye does see.

The trees, strong and tall, are my companions –
my comfort, my joy.

Rivers are twinkling, sparkling and blue,
moving ever so gently ever flowing in you.

Life Goes On

Seashells on the seashore,
an echo like you've felt before.

The spirit world is chanting too,
but do you hear or not want to?

I know and believe that life goes on
beyond the realm of what I see.

A surge of hope pours in on me
as I know that life lasts eternally.

If I Were a Bird

If I were a bird I would love to fly and sit on my perch and not wonder 'why'.

My freedom would take me to wherever I wished, I could look at the world from above, with bliss.

I could waggle my wings and sing a thousand things, share people's gardens and sip from the well.

I could choose my life depending on sight and build my nest amongst the rest of the carefully chosen few.

To see the world from this fair view is something spectacular, and special, it's true.

Get Back to Nature

A century ago life was unchanged, like the pages of a book. Except time has shaken the world into moving faster.

People drive faster, walking, talking – no time for stopping. So they go on the internet, shocked that they're dictated to by screens bleeping and non-stop speaking.

Attached to them like a lifeline, technology convenient but not necessarily a must.

Lets get back to what's important! Find the trust in one another.

Find your way and display yourself creatively. Finding what truly lies within.

Go back to basics, nature and the rest, to enhance your life once more.

Flowers

The flowers are sitting all proudly and sweet.

Ready to be placed in their new home, all neat.

To be loved and tendered to their every need.

To be cherished, nurtured and nourished.

Crystals

So many beautiful crystals, all sparkling and new.

Sending positive energy to everyone anew.

Balancing mind, body and spirit,
to help you on each day.

Cleansing your mind, bringing calmness and kind.

Courage and hope to inspire your day.

The Memories Still Remain

The seagulls made their noise that connected me to the sea, and the smell of salt, and the feel of sand, to bring me back to memories of a child on my summer hols.

A time when life was innocent of problems and full of promises.

To take me to my dreams of a thousand things.

Where possibilities were not impossible, and I could be almost anything I wished to be.

And now that seems to have gone. But not for long as I tune into the song, the sounds of the seagulls.

The memories haven't gone.

A Legacy

We sat on the river, everything slowed.

The water gently rippled as the boats glided and the wind blew.

A peacefulness echoed, a faint sound of bird song in the distance.

Swans bathing, spreading their wings.

The water sparkled like the facets of a diamond ring.

Its purity displaying clarity and substance like the mind, rich in its beliefs.

Someone to rely on, showing truth and not a lie.

When we die a legacy carries on our good name, for generations to come.

Harmony

To be harmonious is to be in tune with yourself and with everything around you.

To feel connected together.

When everything is going smoothly – this is harmony, and there is peace.

The following poems show you what harmony can be, and that, by connecting with your self and your surroundings, you can reach this state of being.

Visualise This & It Goes Like This

The sun was high and the waters running by.

With the feel of something new to get me through.

To another day, when I can say, 'I've done it again!

It's just like heaven when I feel this bliss
and it goes like this:

Orange fills my mind, all golden and sublime.

The skies red too, the horizons still in view.

For a few precious moments, before I rest my head.

I'm taken to a peaceful place where I can dream
and feel supreme.

I open my eyes and take this with me
into a better place.

Where life is free, and it's promised to be.

All golden and beautiful like the sand and the sea.

Stay Happy and True

I sat when the skies were blue,
and I sat when the rain poured through.

My mood stayed the same
no matter whether it rained.

For I had found my tune, set in me,
to stay happy and free.

And I prayed to live an honest life
to be kind and sweet.

To live this life the best I could,
not be greedy, just be good.

And wherever I go, I'll always be true,
true to myself and true to you.

Special Love

The dawn was breaking,
my heart was aching for love of a special kind.

To be loved and cherished especially;
feel beautiful and wanted forever more.

I met my match, he was a good catch,
and mirrored the beauty in me.

The Universe So Radiant

The Universe so radiant – stars sparkling in the sky.

I just look up and see how special the stars are to me.

When I give kindness – it often comes back in the most unexpected ways.

I give a smile to a stranger, and they smile back.

I exchange a kind word - it makes their day, it makes me feel good to be this way.

Life's what you make it; I know this to be true.

The Universe radiates that right back to you!

Working Together

It was time to get back together for everything to be restored. Working together, re-building our lives.

We travelled together, building our homes, gathering wood, working as one.

The children playing happily, no pressure, just fun.

Vegetables we proudly planted, and tended with care, a source of food, with fresh water from the well.

A mixture of thoughts going through my mind – I listened to my heart and knew what I truly wanted.

Special love and understanding, this life we have built together – to keep for generations forever.

My Mother

The bond we share is special and rare.

My thoughts are with you, and are always there.

My heart is with you as I breathe the same air.

You're always in my heart even when we are apart.

The gifts you bring are special too, including your love
that shines right through.

Bringing laughter and joy to all you know – your
company is great to all you see.

Like a special rose all beautiful that glows!

My Father

A man of true strength to aspire to. To look up to and want to be, who shares his love especially.

He's kind and caring, forever sharing.

A true inspiration for all to see, especially for me.

So thank you for your kindness, your special ways, you're one in a million in all your ways.

You bring me happiness, you bring me joy, no words can describe, the love inside.

And most of all the security, that you provide to all.

The Light Has Won!

I turned the corner sheltered and warm, to comfort me
from the harshness of war.

The turmoil within brought me tremor and fear that
only exacerbated more and more.

I looked within to clear this terror – the stormy seas,
the uneasy breeze.

And found within a vision of beauty – a ball of light
that shines so bright!

Displaying all colours in the sky at night.

So wonderful to see!

It seeps out of me, and surges through
to accompany you.

And brings the peace that emanates through.

The darkness has gone, and the light has won!

The Good Old Days

The good old days, we once all knew.

When we had good old English stew.

We sat round the fire, the heart of our home.

To share our woes, all cosy and warm.

And happier times we'd sing together, and laugh out
loud with joy, whatever.

We drove to the seaside – oh what fun!

Sat on the beach and bathed in the sun.

Fish and chips in vinegar, and seaside rock.

None of us bothered to look at the clock!

Paddling in the sea with sand in your toes.

Feeling the salt right up our nose.

Oh, what a joy – a day complete!

An Honesty

The flame was burning brightly in the sky, ready for an emergence of joining together as one.

Balancing our energies to bring peace, and love, stillness; a calm to spread joy through the world.

To calm the storms within each one; who fears and feels no fun.

To hold out your hand in a gesture, to show good will.

I won the key to our heart, as I resolved to start.

Dropping my barriers to enhance my genuineness, and kindness.

Reassuring, not blind to the gestures of good human kind.

Family Time

A new beginning emerges.

The sun shone through, and life carried on in the same old familiar way.

Where children played, and the shops displayed their merchandise, changing from season to season.

At Christmas time – a special time for families, the children waiting patiently for Father Christmas to deliver their parcels.

A time to celebrate together, and love one another.

And when the holidays arrive in the summertime, and the boats come in, they start to grin.

The parks are buzzing, and the children shriek with laughter – for they are free, and it's so much fun just to be!

The clock ticks, time moves on, and the sun shines through once again.

Shared Experiences

Life goes back to normal once more.

We are stronger from our turmoil.

More understanding that we care.

Experiences we never knew.

Have made us stronger too.

And now I know that life can bring such sadness, sorrow, pain and tears.

The depths of my soul have finally reared.

To turn my experiences into something special.

To share with the world my sadness too.

That we can share and treasure with you.

A Special Bond
Amongst Special Friends

A special time amongst special friends, who held me and gave me their loving support on my new venture.

To guide me and steer me, to help me on my way.

To revamp and connect together again – to fuse and hold a special bond, a bond I won't forget.

As I begin my new journey, climb with joy, love, happiness and fulfilment.

Until we meet again!

Symmetry

Look and you will see.

Listen and you will hear.

Be patient, your time will come

And when it does, the sun will shine again
and you will feel alive.

A fresh new perspective you will see,
a new world for you to see.

I changed, and you changed,

I laughed, and you laughed,

I cried, and you cried.

The mirror was in me,
I projected it out for all to see,

A passion, a love so strong; I carried it all along.

Synchronised

Life took on a different song,
it showed me that it could go on.

In spite of what I see, I never expected it to be.

From depression to expression,
from sadness to my dreams.

To give me joy, my heart joins in to the beat of life.

At a rhythm more in time,
that is synchronised.

To smile and laugh, sing out and dance.

It's all in me, as I dance to the
rhythm of the drums in me.

Special Moments

I have taken life to be precious.

To savour every moment as if it will be

my last time to eat, my last time to laugh.

My last time to join with friends and dine,

to share my supper and the wine.

To give all I can, to show my love,

to share special moments, with all I love.

Not to have sorrow, to look forward to tomorrow.

To take life as it should be!

Make it special and be in every moment.

Life brings light to shine eternally!

Our Retreat

Our retreat in the countryside, where our heart is in our home and the kitchen is our main concern to prepare our food and dine.

To connect together all as one, bringing our love – divine from above.

Security we gather together, our thoughts and prayers we share, whatever.

Radiate the peace within, to capture our dreams of special things.

The support, the love we cherish forever.

We thank the heavens for our home together.

My Destiny

I transcended in time to a place in my mind.

A cottage so sweet with the sea and the shore.

And a freedom I adore.

As I let myself go and believe it to be.

My destiny that I deserve and yearn for.

With this wonderful thought, I can go on

And teach hundreds the healing I'd given my life for.

As I evolve, the repercussions are apparent to see.

As it's catching – you'll see.

It spreads like good news, the energies fuse.

To connect one another together.

Happiness

Happiness is being content, and appreciating your life.

It's finding things that make you feel happy.

It's knowing that what you are doing is right.

It's feeling satisfied that you're doing a good job, as good as you can.

Happiness is waking up in the morning, looking forward to the day – not dreading it and hoping time passes away.

Happiness helps me when I'm kind and caring to others.

Happiness is okay even when you're sad – it's a state of mind, a feeling, it helps you even when things are bad.

Once you're happy, it's easier to stay at this level of pure happiness.

Hidden Treasures

My enthusiasm soared, and I sparked and felt overjoyed by life, it's splendour, and what it can bring.

The love of life that truly sings!

The birds join in with praise and sing.

To accompany our hearts and souls and bring

Wonder, for all that you will find.

Hidden in treasures you will find.

The freedom and choice that we are given.

To find your desires that heaven has given.

The power of your voice – it's all your choice.

Encountered Dreams

The orchestra played a beautiful tune that brought tears to my eyes and a flutter to my heart.

The symphony struck a cord in me that filled my mind – with visions of scenes that encountered my dreams.

Of special times I've had when I played in the sea, and the water would be cleansing me.

And the sun would be high and the breeze would flow by, caressing my back,

And warm me through the summer hue, where the skies are always blue.

Connected Together All in a Special Way

We are all connected in a way. We're drawn together by the same breath.

On this plane at the same time.

In a space in time, which so happens to be 2009.

Choosing our paths, learning our skills – all different to merge together to make the world better.

No need for competition as we compliment each other, working together.

Bring us joy, bring us peace, as we work together in one piece – or chaos takes place amongst the human race. Who's going to fix it?

So serve the world in your way, and you've got a chance today!

Connected Together

I showed love, and that would lead the way.

I showed kindness, and they responded back too.

I showed honesty, and I could smile and say,

'I'm true to you'.

I showed sadness, and we shared some tears.

I showed laughter, and we roared away.

I showed that I could be someone, and inspired others too.

I showed they could lean on me, and I could lean on you.

We are all connected in some way.

Angels

I found myself writing a lot of angelic poems, which I have included. This has brought me so much comfort, especially during those times throughout my life when I felt lonely.

I have also found them inspirational. I have been inspired to take on challenges in my life when, previously, I felt fearful at the prospect.

They have given me courage, hope and guidance.

I hope they can be a source of inspiration and comfort to you too – in your sadness, and in your joy.

Security

Angels can bring comfort, warmth, a feeling of calmness and security.

A knowing that everything is going to be all right.

A Helping Hand

A burden I carried for so long – all I needed was to share it, to lighten the load.

Not knowing that anyone would care – on the contrary many did care.

I looked in the right places – they were waiting for me, with arms wide open, to welcome and embrace me.

A smile on my face is all that I needed – and to trust and have faith that all would be well.

My intuition guided me; I could feel their love surrounding me.

To Save the Day

I sent the Angels to give a helping hand to those I love when, in my pain, I couldn't love as much as I would normally do.

Blighted by my pride, I couldn't see what was right or wrong – the choices I see were confused in me, so I prayed for a way to get through.

I asked the skies to justify my choice – to find the way to save the day, and show the way right through –

And, so I say, 'Thank you'.

A Shining Example

Angels glowing, light radiates from their being. We too can shine and be in harmony.

Love one another, bring comfort, bring praise to raise the frequency and we can walk lighter, feel brighter.

Wrap your arms around another to enfold, embrace like the wings of an angel.

Strong, shielding from the fear that can trap and torment our mind.

So take what we see with reverence, be faithful for all our worth.

A shining example of splendour, exuding an air of energy – our grace rare, a uniqueness we can all share.

You Are Not Alone

Thank you for your comfort and the lessons and tests that you bring.

To fight this war until I'm done and show that I can pass the test I'm given.

I'm ready now to give it all back, the experiences from this and that.

I find the Angels serve me well and guide me through, when I'm challenged too.

I have so many people to thank for this, the support and the love that they show.

The Presence of Angels

So kind and caring the Angels flocked over,

A tingling down my spine,

A presence hard to find.

Not lonely, not scared, why would I be?

We shared a special understanding that only they cared.

To reach within, to fight the fear that was only there when I felt bare and lonely, on a journey that seemed rough and tough.

When I opened my heart and my eyes the beauty was there for all to see.

Soft, smooth, gentle, not fierce - like a slow flowing breeze easing me through the pain, I once knew, that was playing in my mind.

Nature took care of that!

The Angels Play Music

The Angels played their music to show how much they cared, and released the fresh smell of flowers that soared up in the air.

As we passed by, unaware that this was their way to show they cared, and tell us that she was still there.

All was calm and peaceful in the air, the Angels relished their mission – to bring comfort to those who have lost loved ones.

The Angels Are Always There

Stormy seas like life's bad dreams.

Rainbow colours, an overwhelming love to replace those bad dreams.

Feathers scattered here and there, to remind me that the angels are always there.

Peace Emanating Through

Peace emanated through from my being, spreading light, transforming darkness into light.

Surging through, reaching out and touching those who wait, to return from their past into a new state, the present time – a moment in time.

To live the life we all once knew, coming back to our home, to start fresh and new.

Bringing Angels and love, laughter and comfort too - to spread the word to all we know.

Joining us together, holding hands forever.

The Angels Sing

The Angels sang from high up above, waiting in the wings just like a Dove.

To cherish, to care, to send love that's so pure.

Their energy refreshing like a cool breeze.

That gets me to ease through the pain.

Magic in the Sky

When the stars sprinkled in the sky.
It was magic of a different kind.

When the skies are dark.
It's a mystery to see.

Where beauty portrays the inner me.
It's in the sky for all to see.

So wondrous and pure like the Angels, you see.
For they are truly part of me!

My Time Would Come

The Angels watched around the clock. They flocked over me when I couldn't see.

When I cleared my head what I could see was a bright reflection of the deep blue sea.

It was peace and quiet on a higher plane and it looked like heaven.

There was no wrong, where the priests and monks called out my name to beckon me to come to thee.

It wasn't my time, so I had to decline and struggled through – to face the truth that my time had not yet come.

It was no coincidence this was my existence.

And when I was ready, then they would come for me.

In Troubled Times

All the joy started to fade away – and then I called upon the Angels who gave me hope and strength to reason with myself.

Their warmth engulfed me, and I felt strength and courage to continue to face the truth – and whatever lay in store.

To fight the fear that seemed so near.

The Angels intervened and lifted my spirits up, and I felt their presence near once more.

Warmth embracing, sending me peace and love.

I Shared My Pain

I thought I'd extricated myself from all the pain till it came back to haunt me once again.

So I took all my courage, my will to survive, to release it once and for all.

With patience, with care, I shared my pain to keep my sanity alive.

While the presence of Angels surrounded me and helped me to stay alive.

The transition gave me a vision to see – of cherry trees, orchards and leaves.

Of a place full of peace, tranquillity and bliss, that stays with me forever more.

Finding Comfort

Your safety net is weighted heavily like a bubble all around, to fit so snugly.

Like the cushions and the pillows of comfort – so soft, white and fluffy like cotton wool.

A replica of Angels keeping a watchful eye.

A source of comfort when lonely... guidance when unsure... tender to lean on when times are tough.

Taking the right path when two paths were there and knowing it felt right.

Believing my purpose.

Encouraging me... a watchful eye to see when there was terror in me.

Angels Comfort

The Angels came to bring you comfort – to free you from your pain and shame.

You did so well – life wasn't fair to you in your turmoil.

An Angel Awaits

Sat waiting for the train through the mist, through the rain.

Vaguely saw a figure replicating an Angel – was it my imagination?

Or was this for real? I blinked and turned to re-adjust and still the figure remained.

Peace spread through like the fog that thickened and surrounded me.

Holding me tight like a glove, to fit and keep me warm from the harm of the threatened storm.

Bereavement

Part of the course of our lives is that we will lose loved ones at some time. When writing these poems I realised that, although I really miss my mother-in-law, she still lives on in me. The true essence of her spirit stays alive, and lives on in all of us that knew her.

I specially wrote some of the following poems for her, and was lucky enough to read them to her before she passed away.

I too wish that these poems will bring you comfort and peace.

The Struggle Had Ended

The inevitable had arrived and she faced the truth and knew what she had to do.

She had fought so strong and no longer could struggle – in this life, at least.

And now she had released all emotional ties and would not compromise – as this journey is over for another to begin.

Exciting and new, beautiful and blue.

Serenity and calm, peaceful with charm.

Golden light soaring at night, so bright.

It's wonderful to see and lovely to be in this place – you'll see.

To Pray

I didn't know how to say goodbye.

No words were spoken and my heart was choking.

Emotions were raw, my tears I cried.

"I love you", I said, "and I'll miss you always".

As I pray for you I take comfort it's true.

It gives me peace and a better life to live,

knowing this is how I can give.

She's At Peace

Thank you for giving me this sign of peace, an echo, a voice much louder; to speak to me to reassure, to comfort in my times of turmoil.

I opened my eyes, not sure what I'd see, and the beauty was vast, and was swirling in me.

It radiates peace, a beautiful calm. I blossomed and felt a wonderful charm.

I was swimming in joy, and it suddenly came to me - that the peace was in me.

Softly Spoken Words

Quiet moments, I'm still and calm. My mind is quiet, words softly speak to me.

She's at peace, no more pain. It's okay to remember all that's good – not the pain.

I know what lives in me, and know how she'll want me to be. I knew her so well.

She brought light, not a shell of empty darkness to dwell in the corners, lurking.

A presence to notice, interesting and kind, involved with the people, the community, so well.

Her thoughts were good, and positive – like they should.

In a Flash

In a flash of time the young grow old and take you to a space in time.

Where they grow wise and their spirits free.

And the sun always rises and captures your heart.

For the beauty's in the world for all to see.

When one life starts, one sets you free to a new place, where the others can't see.

Her True Essence Lives On

Her life has gone – but her energy lives on.

Her energy and essence to be, is in me.

Her humour is witty. Her honesty real.
Her kindness so caring.

She makes me feel special and loved.

And so I live each day in bliss, and know that she
eternally lives.

Eternal Lives

The Angels waited patiently to collect those in pain.

To take them and guide them to a place of peace,
tranquil and kind.

Where elders are wise, and the blind can see, and the
young can grow old and it's promised to be.

No Fighting
No War
No Poverty
No Poor

Where everyone is equal and connected to the core,
the essence of life.

Where the skies are always blue and the sun shines on
you,

And the waters are a reflection of the ever eternal you!

Against All Odds

I lit candles to show how much I love you and show how much I care.

I prayed for you, I prayed for peace, I prayed for your life to give you relief.

Relief from the pain you're suffering too, I couldn't bear even that for you.

You stuck with this and showed it to be true, that life can go on for you.

I believe in the rare possibilities that medical science isn't always right, and that a person has their right to fight.

A tendency that you can't measure, you showed the world you are a treasure!

A Kiss Goodbye

I never had a chance to say goodbye, so in my mind I had to cry.

No one could take that away from me nor the special moments we shared together.

That's in my memory, I'll treasure forever.

To say goodbye, I know it's true that I can send that through to you.

Distance and time and energy, no one can stop it, you just can't block it.

I've faced the truth, I'll let you go to a better place that you will know.

Your energy goes on forever, and the true essence of you is splendid and new in another body, that's better too.

An Inspiration

Tired and bruised from the turmoil
– who cares in the end?

What matters is this:

The person in question – important to me,
the whole point of our pain,
our grieving, our crying, our laughing.

Of memories we keep.

She fought to the end, that strength I will find.
Her nature, her ways were brilliant.

An inspiration to me.

Faith

Having faith plays a big part in life's process.

Believing in ourselves takes real courage.

On our journey in life there are difficult challenges and events that happen, which sometimes we have no control over.

I have written some inspirational pieces of writing to show you just how faith can pull you through.

I have many experiences that have shown me that, with trust and courage, faith will come. Faith will show you a way through.

Who is God?

God is in me.

God is in everything I see.

God is what I aspire to.

God is my shining light, my goal, my role, my joy.

Believe In Yourself

Stars so bright to guide your way, your purpose, your true path.

My focus solid, I don't let it rock, my ambitions and dreams are a time tunnel – when I take my slot.

I relished the moment and breathed in the air, to remember this, this feeling of bliss.

I have faith and believe in what I can achieve.

The Resurrection

My heart was bleeding from the pain; my time was near to die for the people I had to save from the lies. To conquer all and bring peace and love, not war.

I was frightened, it was torture. I cried out in pain and asked for the answers but nothing came.

Then in the darkness all was still, no-one came to get me until – the light shone bright and a hand held me tight, to take me to a place that was comfort and still.

As I sat with my father it all came to me, while he gave me this gift to set us all free. Free from slavery, free from pain.

To follow my death, I had to go back to finish the work I had set out to do, to lead the country and bring good; amongst all the trouble and the toil.

Happiness spread through from a chosen few, who carried out the word of joy from their hearts.

A Bright Golden Flame

I moved out of the path of destruction.

My heart twinged with pain, my brain was in pieces like broken crockery that needed putting back together.

With all my strength I prayed for peace, for a helping hand in order to keep my sanity and wisdom.

To know that I believe in right from wrong, and the situation wasn't ideal all along.

I had to escape in order to make my decision to stand my ground.

To continue the path of righteousness, of all my dreams that I put on hold, until the time that I got told, your time is now.

Don't give in to the pain. Non-existent, it's only a short resistance to hold you back against the true forces of nature.

So forge on ahead, break through, don't feel dead when you feel beaten and dread the day ahead.

Take action. Get back on track. Hold the torch, a bright golden flame.

Hope Prevails

A golden light was emerging from me, filling me with warmth like the burning flames of the fire, warm, cosy, glowing.

Hope prevails – they're all waiting for me to join this new wondrous journey.

Where the skies are blue and flowers too, have new meaning in their lives.

Open flowers, an open heart to start the day and give in to a way like never before.

Offering your love spreads like wild flowers – to those who wait in anticipation.

Sitting in the darkness in wonder – whether they can find the strength to move forward, to find hope somewhere.

So I say, 'I can give to you' since I once knew, how that felt too.

I'm sorry to see your anguish, the same as I once knew.

I Make the Best of What I Have

I can make the best of what I have, and fight for peace in this world of troubles.

I can move to the music that resides in me, and go with my heart, and the world I see.

I can make the most of what I have, and turn it into gold, because that's what I see.

I can love with my heart – that gives me joy, and embrace what I have, for evermore.

I Trusted & Love Showed
Me the Way

Death stared me in the face – nowhere to run.

I had to face the truth.

I gave up and put my trust in those who cared.

I believed what they said was for the best, and that
they knew the right way through.

My will to live, was stronger then if I chose to die –
then what would there be?

I hadn't lived long enough to see.

My child, so precious, I wanted to see her grow up in
front of me.

And so I live to tell the tale!

With Faith & Trust I Can Believe

With Love in my heart, I can achieve anything.

With Trust, I will go a long way, and build great relationships.

With Prosperity, I will live in my joy comfortably, without worry.

With Hope, I can achieve my dreams.

With Laughter, I can bring happiness into my life and the lives of others.

With Tears, I shed all my sadness.

With Faith, I can believe in myself and others, and live a happy and fulfilling life.

Vitality

I took the path with courage, not fear.

My determination intense.

With faith to make my life so full of plenty.

Like a tree when the fruit ripens and leaves multiply, bursting with life and vitality.

Surging, heading for the sun, that gives energy to everyone.

Radiant; glowing and glorious from all the joy.

The energy exuberant trapping goodness; lifting me up with an air of radiance.

A wonderful presence – the Angels are above.

Those Times Are Gone...

Those times are gone... when I couldn't speak and only weep.

When the days were long, and I didn't want to go on.

When the urgency inside was to feel more alive.

When the darkness hung thick over my head.

When there was no laughter left in me.

Now, all I see are colours so strong and a strength to carry on.

Excitement like I've never felt before.

A knowing, a confidence, having faith and trust that my path is right.

And the cause that I fight for is worthy for me.

The Tides Had Turned

I stood in quiet thought waiting for the others to rise, reflecting on my life, and the changes that had occurred.

My mind was in a whirl, as I tried to make sense of these changes in my life.

Oh! But great changes, where the tides had turned, and my heart yearned for more excitement than I'd ever had before.

Where I floated on my dreams; I would never have believed, that this could really happen to me.

Decisions were made to change my life forever, and give me great pleasure.

The tides had turned, the pathways had opened, and the waves changed their direction.

Hope

Thank you for this day – I'm blessed.

I'm grateful and I'll do my best.

To help all those to find their happiness.

They've struggled for so long.

And now it's time to make some changes.

A simple formula, and that's called love.

A tonic, that comes from the heart.

To Believe Once Again

I tried to rid myself of the pain, but didn't know how to find the way.

I was guided and confided, and still the answers never came.

Then one day it all began to unravel itself, like a rope, that had held me tight.

It fell into place piece by piece, like a jigsaw that knew its place.

I took faith, to believe, and managed to go on, to find my way out of this maze.

As time went by, I started to believe in myself once again.

The Beauty in the Sea

I acquainted myself with the sea, the sound of the waves as it splashed on the shore.

The crunching of pebbles beneath my feet, and the beauty in the beach.

To show me what life can be, to find myself once more.

When I was lost and lonely – like the shore in stormy seas, when it's abandoned by the breeze.

The same as I felt, when not sheltered, not safe, not warm.

Not knowing if it would come to the end, so I planned to end my life; but this wasn't meant to be, and my life changed accordingly.

It was worth it in the end, all the pain, and the suffering that finally amends.

The Key to Unlock the Door

I was drifting once more, until I saw what seemed to be a plan.

I pieced it together bit by bit, and found that it could go like this –

People staring right at me, were giving me a signal to find the key.

The key to unlock my destiny – it was obvious when I looked inside of me.

I asked a question, it went like this – "what's my next step?"

I found that this was to be loving and kind and caring to all mankind.

It became a privilege – this way to be, that opened the door and gave me the key, to more opportunities awaiting me.

The Comfort of Others

The comfort of others who care and share.

A source of something, I find so rare.

To give to others in such a way.

To love and share these gifts, I pray.

I give thanks for being in this position – as once the roles were reversed, and I looked up to the nurse.

To trust in her, as she in me, so I found my way... a miracle I see.

Now when I look back, it was special to me, a part of my life, a gift – I see.

Stay True

In all my sadness and confusion, I hoped for a way to get through.

Not believing that the truth would set me free.

Then a triumph occurred, and the tables turned, for the better for me.

In all my doubt I didn't shout, kept calm and true.

Now feel free from the pain that grew.

The path is clearer; and it's all much nearer,

To embrace my life once more.

My vision is strong. I feel I can go on.

I took faith in both hands and was strong in my beliefs.

This pulled me through to the end.

Reach Out To Give
A Helping Hand

Reach out to others when they feel lost and lonely, not knowing where to turn on their long and winding journey.

Why not ease their pain and give a helping hand to nudge them on their way?

Give, and you will receive an amazing energy of love and goodness that fills you up with excitement, releasing more good.

Prevail and inhale a haze of sunshine shimmering through, to shine on you.

Triumphant, anew!

No Regrets

The darkness drew in, as the light slipped away, for another day to begin.

I felt sadness as I looked back, and saw many regrets in my life.

So I pulled myself back to the present time, to dust myself off.

I took a big gulp, and carried on to face the day.

I took the lessons I have learned, and used them in a better way, and found some wisdom from the disarray.

Life is Pleasure

What could be better than a life full of pleasure?

A love so strong like the flowing breeze, gentle on your face, like a warm embrace.

Together we can make it, our lives entwined like the Russian vines that wrap themselves around, and take hold from the ground.

That brings us strength, and meaning to our lives.

To find the way – your place in life, without the strife.

Pluck out the old; make room for the good, the fresh air will ripen with care.

To bloom and open; as our heart resumes.

Justice

I can smile with satisfaction as times gone by.

I fought for peace, for justice to keep my family safe, from the heartache and injustice of it all.

The tables have turned, and kindness returned.

The pain and suffering has gone, replaced with rare precious gifts – that's enriching, and gives me the love I deserve.

I can be proud on this earth.

Have Faith

Happiness is a feeling that I can grasp at any time.

It's always there even when I'm in the depths of despair.

When the waves wash over me and I have trouble to see.

To see my way out of a tragedy, and when the waves settle down, I no longer feel I drown.

I can cope beyond any measure and look the world in the eye.

Fear is no longer near, as faith becomes my guide, my steer.

Grow With Time

I wondered lonely as a child to seek my vision, my fulfilment, my need.

Without any faith, I had to escape and took the wrong road for a while.

I travelled along, looking in all the wrong places for something to grasp.

As if I was blind, I searched for my soul – my wisdom would come with time.

So I trudged along, still carrying on, not able to see in front of me.

Years passed by, the pain inside I carried so long from trusting, and not knowing, mistaking my judgement.

When I denied to face the truth, and see it for what it was.

Then all of a sudden the tables turned, I chose my vocation and started to learn.

A whole new world I started to see.

That brings me peace, and makes sense to me.

Enriched with Gold

I'm enriched with gold that shines from me;
it's a blessing in disguise that I couldn't see.

Faced with death, pain and sorrow that I couldn't bear,
for the next day – tomorrow.

Till my life took a turn, that gradually healed,
and promised me it was worth the fight.

Hope brought courage, and courage brought light,
that opened the way to take on the fight.

To continue this life, and so I can see,
a golden pathway; all lit up for me!

Experiences to Treasure

I stilled my mind as peace flowed through.

I accepted the situation as best I could.

To embrace it and nurture my needs, to stay calm in stormy seas.

To send love to everyone, to find comfort in the sun.

The warmth envelops me, to re-energise and caress my feelings - that would otherwise feel dull.

I rise above, and forge ahead, taking courage for this day that I somehow could dread.

I find peace instead, to encompass my experiences to treasure – to add to my experiences forever.

Don't Fight the Stormy Seas

I'd love to go back to a time when sailors wore their caps, and captains had the eye for steering the ship, keeping their crew safe under their watchful eye.

The women don't deny that they miss their beloveds as the ship sails by; they are proud to be the wives of sailors, who have courage and strength to honour their country.

Waving frantically at the docks. The ship steers out on its course, ready to embark on its journey.

We, too, have our journey across the seas. Facing challenges and obstacles – to test our strengths to deal with life, so like the sea, a calm day when it's settled and a gentle breeze cools the air.

Or a stormy day, when the wind is high, emotions running high, the waves bashing to and fro. Don't you know – it doesn't have to be this way?

So, go with the currents don't fight the other way, it makes the journey smoother this way.

Then you will see the horizon, when the sun sets in the sky, and the birds glide beautifully above you.

Courage

I search through my feelings that were deep within me
– to find the one that will set me free.

To picture myself feeling happy and free.

I tried to imagine somewhere where I can feel joy and
laughter – but really I know; I can't run from me.

So I face it full on, the day and beyond.

With courage, to stay with me.

Be Thankful

Life has pleasures in many different ways.

Unexpected gifts can often come your way.

There's so much we can do,
and so much we can choose.

So, be thankful for each and every day.

A Step of Faith

I took the step I dreaded all along,

It wasn't what I'd thought.

Not scary, not fearful, but extremely exhilarating – full of energy, like the sun.

A big ball of fire charged with happiness and joy bursting at the seams.

A smile I couldn't wipe off my face.

A spring in my step I rarely felt before – an excitement about life I hadn't had before.

I'd been conditioned over the years to believe that this step would be fatal, negative, a failure.

It's not true!

Believe in yourself and your dreams will come true.

Awaken to Hope

I awoke with hope, a new day to cope.

My spirits were lifting and my thoughts had been drifting away from my mind.

I take comfort in memories that I can hold dear, my heart is full of love – a pleasure so near.

Surging mountains far to climb with courage, not fear – I manage to steer.

To hold out my hand to show how I care, your beauty surrounds us and the love that we share.

Inspiration

Whenever I have a challenge or project of some sort, this encourages me and stimulates me to explore my creative self.

I have surprised myself as to what I can achieve.

It's both exciting and exhilarating, and when you are inspired you can reach great heights.

Your true self can really shine through.

What Comes Next?

I walked with confidence and grace as I knew my place.

I took faith in both my hands and knew my next step would be planned.

No need to worry or fear.

Inspired by this, I couldn't resist, so I journeyed along to carry on.

No longer forlorn, I had courage and strength.

As I carried along the path that shone; and opened a new way for me.

I was surging along – my power so strong, and the fear had gone.

Replaced with a love so strong, to fight, to carry on.

Giving

It takes time, and time is what I've got.

Life gave me this; in which to choose how I use

these precious gifts.

So I sift through all my things, until the time has

come to bring – to all of those my compassion, my

wisdom from learning.

My passion, my yearning to give in this life.

Joy In My Heart

It's taken me to a further plane, I wobbled at first and now I've rehearsed.

I'm as fine as can be, it's amazing to see, and the pleasure from this gives me joy and bliss.

I hug myself, and pinch myself that life can be this!

No Matter What

No matter what, you're all stars in my eyes;
you prove to me there's no compromise.

Forget the grades – you're all straight A's
– to me a prodigy.

You're shining through from the praise I gave you.

You are all amazing stars in my eyes.

The Beauty in Us All

We moved forward. As one life ends and another begins and in the meantime our lives keep moving, until life ends.

So I take each day as precious and say, "thank you for this", the treasure and the gifts, hidden in ways that I didn't see.

In all the creatures, great and small and in the beauty of us all.

In the skies and in the trees, and in the birds and in the bees.

And the rays of sunlight when they hit the trees – that shine on my face in the cool summer breeze.

The colours in the rainbows when the raindrops fall, and the feel of emotions when I fall.

But most of all, I thank the world for giving me a place in this world once more.

To Fight For the Truth

I searched around for a home for a while. When all along it was in front of me.

I took what I had, made plans, made a bed to lie on and comfort me.

Then I searched for the truth, and was inspired by people I never thought I would have found, in the world I thought was empty and full of the perils that life could bring.

There was kindness there for all to share, if I let it bear, like a fruit to share.

If I make it possible to fight the cause and make the choice for freedom, of course.

My Imagination

I transcended into a place in my mind.

A beautiful cottage, all pretty and safe. White flowers embraced around the garden gate.

My inner-self was gratified, as I could visualise this place in me - to one day be my reality.

It helps me to survive, to feel more alive, to cope with the stress, to imagine the best!

True Friends

When we were lonely on our journey we always had each other near, just never knew your face revealed.

Your energy, I had once known from other lives we have since perceived.

And so fate has it we crossed paths and, on sight, fused again once more.

And, as we walk together side by side, we never have anything to hide.

We share our dreams, our tears, our fears.

For now, as friends we have each other to guide and love and support, whatever.

Time Changes Things

Depression hung over my head like a dark cloud following me around. I couldn't shake it off, this dread.

Then, all of a sudden I turned the corner . . . in spite of this I started to alter.

My body, my mind seemed to change in time, and turn around in spite of my life.

Life had been hard at times and gradually, happiness took over, and joy set in.

An excitement and thrill for living, just like when winter has been and spring comes to life.

I felt blessed and loved to see this sight, and have the chance for success.

Survival Mode

Suppressed emotions bubbled to the surface.

I dealt with them as best I could,
to find the source deep down inside.

My instinct to survive made me feel more alive.

Like climbing a hill,
when you reach the top it evens out.

Not such a shock as you see much clearer.

And it's all much nearer to
embrace yourself once more.

As the memories become more distant, to fade away.

The feelings disintegrate,
what's left is a knowing so strong.

That the fight to survive was worth the ride.

And the price to pay for the pain endured.

Now the energy in your aura has grown
so strong that it cannot alter.

Inspiration an Amazing Thing

Inspiration, an amazing thing that springs up unexpectedly. It lifts me up to a plateau that's high, and I just want to fly.

The universe feeds back the info when I'm in this place of hierarchy.

My abilities soar, it's not such a chore for my creative side to emerge from the floor, and up through me with glee.

As I turn my hand into something special, rare and grand!

Home

My cottage stood tidy, cosy and inviting. My home of bliss, safe and warm, to bring me back from my treacherous journey to an inner peace and quiet.

To release my life from all the strife and share these things, these precious gifts I bring, with those who've suffered from a thousand things.

My life has changed; I am amazed. I thank God too for what he had to do, in order to make my path of sorrow and pain so true.

And now my life is splendid and filled with beauty, love and laughter!

Golden Hoops & Fields of Gold

I played my favourite tune and felt that I would bloom.

I climbed the mountain up so high and felt that I would fly.

No longer ever looking back, serves no purpose and with that;

I take my lessons that I've learned.

Have wisdom, and more choices to discern.

Life no longer gets me down.

I worked harder, changed my course, was willing to take risks and dive and turn.

I jumped like this, through golden hoops and fields of gold.

Where beauty holds the radiant colours, shining from the skies.

My love, my life to be, so possible – it's plain to see.

Golden Sunlight

Golden sunlight brings me hope and peace, and warmth to keep.

The wind cools the air, and softens the heat to bring me fresh air.

My heart warms in me as the beauty I see makes me feel so alive. I thank God that I am alive.

To carry my dreams and cherish my memories.

To remember all the good things that have kept me alive.

And the difficult times, that I'd had to face, have given me hope, and a way to cope - to pass on to others this golden experience.

Get Back On Track

I hibernated all winter, was lonely and forlorn.

I lost the sight, my will, my fight. Felt negative and a dread, of what lay ahead.

In need of help, I found my dream; was back in focus.

And what it seemed that I could glean from this experience, was – don't lose your sight, or lose the fight to find your inner light!

A Choice to Make

She met the crossroads, she changed her course, and decided there was a choice.

A choice to live, to breathe this air that we all share.

We're all connected together as one.

So, in her pain, I felt it too. I understood what she was going through, in my own way – I have to say.

I too had faced the inevitable truth of life or death, and decided to fight – for I had no sight of wanting to end my life.

I admire her strength, her positive ways, she has so much in so many different ways.

She showed me hope when all else fails, an inspiration that tells the tale.

Positive Thoughts

A great way to start the day!

Affirming positive thoughts releases good constructive energy within and around you and always seems to help the day. I inevitably feel happier and stronger for whatever lies ahead.

On the follow page are a few of my favourite affirmations that you can say out loud or to yourself.

Repeat each one three times. Choose one at a time if you wish, believing each word as you say it.

Believe Each Word

- I am having a wonderful day, I know it to be this way.

- The sun is always shining, even when it's hidden behind a cloud.

- I am always loved.

- Each day I do my very best.

- I am happy, the world is happy.

- It's not what I see, it's how I see it.

- The beauty stays always.

Savour the Moment

My outlook is glossy, my future is bright.

When I stay in the moment, I can relish the light.

Not thinking too far forward, nor thinking too far back.

I allow in the moment, to savour the emotions, the feelings I can bear.

The power of this, takes the fear away – it allows me pleasure to face the day.

Portray Your Light

Portraying my light, showed me that I can be calm, and lead the way.

Light shines from us all – let it flow, let it soar.

Rich, golden, full of lustre, that hands to others the golden key.

To unlock the self, it motivates and drives your needs.

It gives attention, let Divine intervention lead the way.

And you will portray your light!

A Place in Me

Thank you for your shining light, it's always burning ever so bright.

Eternally a pleasure to see, it keeps me strong and takes me beyond, to a place that I always had in me.

A place where my dreams are my possibilities, to be anything I want to be, and have courage to be.

This light that I have is sparkling in me, this treasure I have, gives me certainty – a security, a knowing so strong that I'm heading in the right direction.

Empowerment

My entire journey and all the life experiences that I have written about in this book, have led me to a strength within, to a place of wisdom.

I decided to close the book with a section on *Empowerment* because I believe it's a triumph to be able to stand strong in your beliefs, to have the confidence to carry this with you – throughout your life.

A Precious Economy

Every second, minute, hour my body re-oxygenates and showers me with golden light.

Replenishing, refreshing, replicating cells to kick start my system into automatic pilot, when all systems are go.

I am a precious economy, more than the eye can see.

Technology needed in the world today, but it won't beat me and take me over.

I gaze outwards and look to nature, for my comfort, for my joy.

To lift up my spirits, and make my heart soar.

I know that every step I take, a force will show me the way to go.

I know and believe this to be true.

For All My Worth

I kept hold of my worth, a priceless piece – like a painting with its rare intricacies, each detail traces a mark of true excellence.

I hold close to my heart my specialities that I can share, when the time comes to spread the words with meaning from my heart.

Chosen to tread carefully, as trust creeps in gradually, and my instinct jolts me to be aware, as I hold this sacred and precious key.

Remember that's from me, and that my word is faithful and true!

You Are Special

On my pilgrimage across the seas.

The skies were innumerable – protesting to be, invisible from the rays of sunlight to spread across the world.

Shining on you, each and every one of you, as you are a child of God - important, special, unique, with gifts that God has given you.

Your light is always shining; like a magic wand, although at times it needs re-igniting.

So, keep alive and know you are exceptional!

When a Child is Born

It was in the small hours a child was born, an heir to the throne that was unknown at the time of his birth.

His mother cradled her bundle, a comfort and joy; as the bond took place with each small embrace.

A smile on her face, as she knew her place in life, and what lies ahead for her son, when he reached his chosen place.

He sat on the throne, the crowd looked up in adoration as the jewels displayed shone brightly from the rays of sunlight, to bring bliss from all of this.

Be proud, sit on your throne, let the crowd be your chosen friends, your family, your Beau.

Take precedence, for all you know you stand for, your beliefs, with confidence to share, to all of those who care.

The Power Within

I walked along the path so strong

The barriers had finally gone

The door flicked open, I finally could see

A new horizon in front of me

The energy coaxing me, goading me on

An excitement welling inside of me

As my confidence grew, I was stronger each day

I believed in myself and what I had to say

To reach out to others, to show how I cared

To make all the difference with kindness and care.

Treasure Your Uniqueness

Cloudless sky, blue vast, expansive – as we all are.

Not always reaching our full potential, but knowing

That it's there, to bear and raise our limits – extraordinarily high.

Beyond the normal measure.

Treasure your gifts.

A uniqueness that's full of bliss.

On Stage

Think of yourself as if you were going out on stage

The audience applaud you

You're in the spotlight

You're amazing and loved

The fire burning within you

You fly like a dove.

True Talents

No matter who you are

No matter where you are

Your true talents will shine through,

when you believe in you.

The Will to Survive

I struggled along with the will to survive, the power to stay alive.

With strength, with courage, with all my might, I didn't give up the fight.

I must have known that all along, deep down inside, my goal, my dreams would have to be – to save the souls of all who've lost their way.

The Answers Were
There All Along

I searched my soul to find the truth,

to fill the purpose in my life.

I meditated, I prayed, I cried, felt lonely and sad.

I searched for answers but to no avail, till I suddenly realised the answers were there all along.

It took time. I trusted my time would come.

I need look no further.

They were right here, right now, they were within me.

The Truth Will Set You Free

Your kindness and care helped others from the fix, but you took the brunt and burden of this.

You carried a weight so heavily on your shoulders, you took the blame and carried the shame.

Until the day of judgement when your time will come.

You rose again and you gradually felt lighter, and the stars shone brighter over you.

Your heart was set free, as the lies that were told started to finally unfold.

And the guilt that you took and the anger that shook - was disappearing slowly away into a mist, in a haze.

As justice prevailed, and the truth finally set you free!

The Angels,
Looking Down On You

High on the rooftops looking down on me, I'm not alone as I can see, Angels embracing – oh, so softly.

Just waiting and watching to lead me on, so I gathered my thoughts to send my love to those I cared and shared, and gave compassion to those I didn't know.

I kept patient and still to find my skill, to serve my purpose with all my will.

Start with your home to build solid and firm, your empire so strong, to carry you along.

My Intuition

My intuition guided me and I was always especially aware of what my feelings showed, and the love in my heart really flowed.

My passion for life had given in to strife and I couldn't find my way for a while, when all I had to say was "why?"

Then I discovered the secret that lay within, a beauty and love I could only bring.

I searched my soul and found the thing that I'd really lost for a while.

It starts like this and feels like bliss – a buzz in my heart, a surge of light, an energy so new it blossoms right through.

The colours it brings are bright and blue, and sparkle through - I'm so lucky too!

My Better Judgement

My guide was my inner guide, my wisdom was within.

I had the true answers that only lie within.

Blocking out externally, to gain the truth to set me free from the turmoil and confusion that suffocated me.

I followed through my better judgement; that only came from experiences gained by the tests and the rest of society, that at the time felt like an enemy against me.

If only I had known I was my own worst enemy!

So I jacked it in, and found the thing that lies within.

True love, once and for all, to stay strong and tall.

Follow it through and you will feel new – a fresh new beginning sizzling through.

Fresh, like snowdrops on a morning dew.

A True Warrior

I'm powerful. A Goddess. A true Warrior.

I stand tall, have faith and beliefs. I stand for what I believe to be kind, to be true.

I wander through the thick dense forest, not knowing what lies ahead.

Keeping my senses all about me, tuning into my senses, keeping my instincts alive to survive.

Aware of a crackle of a twig, or the crunching of leaves. To warn me of danger that could drive me off my path, to a place I don't know.

To deter me from my destination, my focus, my striving to actualise.

To reach my goals, my full potential, my emotions alive as I find my path, my purpose, my way.

Reflections in the Sea
& All That's in Me

I stand tall – calm, serene, my hair flowing in the breeze.

Looking out to sea, having lived the life of my dreams.

I'm accomplished, have made it further then I ever would have imagined.

My heart soars with laughter and love, bursting and beaming with joy.

My experiences that were hard to bear, are behind me now, no longer a fear in me.

Long since gone, and what's left is a richness that bears the resemblance of a shining star.

Lined with gold, shimmering and sparkling on the sea.

As the waves ripple gentle and calm, like they feel in me.

Final Thoughts

Being creative through writing has given me the strength and courage to believe in myself.

The power of these inspirational words has helped me to overcome my fears, enabling me to believe that anything is possible.

Throughout my journey faith and trust have shown me the way forward, allowing my thoughts and my energy to remain positive, which, in turn, has attracted even more good into my life.

Now, every day for me is special and a gift!

I wish you a happy, fulfilling and prosperous life.

I hope that you have found your true passion in life, and are able to connect with your inner-self and everything around you – to inspire your dreams and enhance your creative abilities.

This state of being carries the potential to balance your mind, body and spirit and enable you to feel more harmonious, more peaceful.

I sincerely hope this book inspires you to reflect upon your life, to take time for yourself, relax and meditate on its contents.

Find your inner peace – as I have found mine, and your inner light will shine through!

About the Author

Liz Everett is a Reiki and Anusha Master Teacher and Healer. She has Diplomas in Counselling and Indian Head Massage, and has dedicated her life to helping others.

Liz worked in the Youth Service for many years, counselling and supporting teenagers. In that time she attended a considerable number of workshops and training programmes to support her work.

She has the ability to work at a very deep level with her clients, and possesses a remarkable understanding and empathy towards people because of her wealth of knowledge and life experiences.

Liz also runs workshops, incorporating her inspirational writings, to help others to re-ignite their creative selves - bringing out their unique gifts.

For more details on Liz's inspirational workshops, and healing:

Visit her website:
www.ladybirdlodge.me.uk

Or please feel free to email Liz at:
liz@ladybirdloge.me.uk

lįp

ATTENTION WRITERS

Do you want to get published?

LIP wants to work with new Authors in the fields of self-help, health, healing, mind body & spirit and personal development.

We want to help you turn your creative work into a reality.

We make publishing fast, easy and fun! And we help you live the dream by getting your books, e-books, CDs and MP3s published and distributed across a global network.

For more information visit our website at:

www.liveitpublishing.com

LIP... The easiest way to get published!

Lightning Source UK Ltd.
Milton Keynes UK
20 November 2009

146510UK00001B/68/P